pharmakon

TELEMORPHOSIS

Jean Baudrillard

TELEMORPHOSIS

preceded by

DUST BREEDING

Univocal

L' Élevage de poussière and *Télémorphose*
by Jean Baudrillard © 2001 Sens & Tonka

Translated by Drew S. Burk
as *Dust Breeding* and *Telemorphosis*
First Edition
Minneapolis © 2011, Univocal Publishing

Published by Univocal
123 North 3rd Street, #202
Minneapolis, MN 55401

Thanks to Meredith Wagner, John Ebert, Hubert Tonka,
Jeanne-Marie Sens, Sylvère Lotringer and Marine Baudrillard

Designed & Printed by Jason Wagner

Distributed by the University of Minnesota Press

ISBN 9781937561000
Library of Congress Control Number 2011935981

INTRODUCTION

Our entire reality has become experimental. In the absence of any stable destiny, modern man has reached the point of unlimited experimentation on himself.
- Jean Baudrillard

The art of living today has shifted to a continuous state of the experimental.

In one of his last texts, *Telemorphosis,* renowned thinker and anti-philosopher Jean Baudrillard takes on the task of thinking and reflecting upon the coming digital media architectures of the social. While "the social" may have never existed, according to Baudrillard, his analysis at the beginning of the 21st century of the coming social media networked cultures cannot be ignored. One need not look far in order to find oneself snared within some sort of screenification of a techno-social community. "What the most radical critical critique, the most subversive delirious imagination, what no Situationist drift could have done… television has done." Collective reality has entered a realm of telemorphosis.

Baudrillard stares down what he identifies as the telemorphosis of reality within a culture, taken prisoner by its own fascination with itself: this cinematic *coup d'état* of the imaginary and the real, where banality and its celebratory status capture us all within self-referential spectacles of life and death. In a social mediated universe of parallel worlds of doubled up delirium between reality and its theatrical double, the screen, Jean Baudrillard's insights into the political, social, and cultural structures of the 21st century and its relationship to media have only begun to resonate with such anticipatory richness, that any thinker or cultural theorist today must have the courage to read (or return to) this prophetic thinker at the edge of the coming age of singularities, networks, and technical image production.

Reality television and more importantly its digital offspring such as social networking sites like Facebook or Google+ have led to a theatricality and fascination with banality that now more than ever needs to be taken seriously as mechanisms of individuation, self-surveillance, and the restructuring of desire become turned into carnival attractions of the highest order and we find ourselves returning to Spinoza's famous question: of what is the body capable?

The political body, the social body, and digital body, all collectivities of the human today must pass through this telemorphosis of the screen.

> We've become individuated beings: non-divisible with others or ourselves. This individuation, which we are so proud of, has nothing to do with personal liberty; on the contrary, it is a general promiscuity. It is not necessarily a promiscuity of bodies in space - but of screens from one end of the world to the other. And it is probably screen promiscuity that is the real promiscuity: the indivisibility of every human particle at a distance tens of thousands of kilometers - like millions of twins who are incapable of separating from their double. Umbilicus limbo.

Umbilicus limbo. Artaud. The theatre and its double. Today we all dance the tango of the onscreen double. Baudrillard reminds us again that if one wants to avoid the traps of reality, one must "move faster than it." And, as usual, Baudrillard's gaze accelerates faster than reality.

> *There will soon be nothing more than self-communicating zombies, whose lone umbilical relay will be their own feedback image - electronic avatars of dead shadows who, beyond death and the river Styx, will wander, perpetually passing their time retelling their own story.*

Yes, Jean, we know. We know the shadow stories are still singing. The encapsulation and self-confinement of the age of the screen world, even in its most mobile formats, becomes a reminder once again of the ecstasy of communication where everything is said, everything forgotten and where no one is speaking the same language.

Everyone knows that reality shows are edited image-scenarios, framed within a

XIII

pre-fabricated context in order to elicit certain responses and fascination from the audience. But as we enter headlong into a media-sphere where everything arrives with a built-in banality switch, we find the scenario trickling its way into every aspect of existence. Reality's desire is to bathe in the banality of its own image feedback, and in achieving this it becomes hostage of its own feedback image. We must have the courage to rigorously question our own relationship to the deliriums of the self-referential closed-circuit exchanges. We must attempt to liberate ourselves from our own fascination with the lowest common denominator of existence: the banality of existence itself.

- Drew S. Burk

DUST BREEDING

DUST BREEDING

Our entire reality has become experimental. In the absence of any stable destiny, modern man has reached the point of unlimited experimentation on himself.

Two recent illustrations of this can be seen: *Loft Story*[1], the mediated illusion of the presentation of the real as "live". The other case is the story of Catherine Millet[2], who provides the phantasmatic illusion of "live" sex.

---

1 *Loft Story* is the French adaptation of the T.V. reality show, *Big Brother*.
2 Catherine Millet is the author of an autobiographical book detailing her sex life from childhood up until adulthood. Some critics have called her account the most explicit book on sex written by a woman.

3

Loft Story is, of course, a concept that has become universally accepted: a condensed version of a human amusement park, ghetto, solitary confinement, and Exterminating Angel. Voluntary reclusion as a laboratory of synthetic conviviality, of telegenetically modified sociality.

It is here, when everything has been given over to viewing (as in *Big Brother* and the other reality shows) that one perceives that there is nothing left to see. It is the mirror of flatness, of the zero degree, where, contrary to all objectives of a real which the show claims to show, it becomes the proof of the disappearance of the other, and perhaps even the fact that the human is not a social being. The equivalent of a readymade - an unchanged transposition like that of *everyday life,* which is itself already rigged by all the dominant models.

A synthetic banality, fabricated within a closed circuit and under a controlled screen.

In this manner, the artificial microcosm of *Loft Story* is identical to Disneyland, which provides the illusion of the real external world, while if one looks deeper, one realizes they are one and the same. The entire United States is Disneyland and we are all on *Loft Story*. No need to enter into the idea of the virtual double of reality, we are already there - the televisual universe is nothing more than a holographic detail of global reality. All the way up to, and including, the most daily parts of our existence, we are already within a situation of experimental reality. And it is precisely from this that we have the fascination, by immersion, of spontaneous interactivity. Are we dealing with a porno voyeurism?

No. Sex can be found everywhere, but it is not what people want. What they profoundly desire is the spectacle of banality, which today has become the real pornography, the real obscenity - of nothingness, insignificance, and flatness. The complete opposite of the *Theatre of Cruelty*. But perhaps there is a form of cruelty which can be seen there as well, at least a virtual one. At a time when television and the media are less and less capable of accounting for the (unbearable) events of the world, they discover daily life, existential banality as the most deadly event, as the most violent actuality, even as the site of the most perfect crime. And actually... it is. And people are fascinated, fascinated and terrified by the indifference of the Nothing-to-say, Nothing-to-do, by indifference to their own existence. The contemplation of the Perfect Crime, of banality as a new vision of fatality, has become a real Olympic discipline, or the last avatar of extreme sports.

All of this is reinforced by the fact that the public is itself mobilized as judge, that it has itself become Big Brother. We are way beyond the panopticon, of visibility as the source of power and control. It is no longer about rendering things visible to the external eye, but rendering them transparent to themselves, via a perfusion of control within the masses, and in erasing any trace of the operation. So it is that the spectators are implicated in a gigantic negative counter-transfer of themselves, and once again, it is from this situation that we see the dizzying attraction of this spectacle.

In the end, all of this comes from the desire to be Nothing and to be looked at as such. There are two manners of disappearing: either we demand not to be seen (this is the current problem concerning image rights), or we immerse ourselves in the delirious exhibitionism of its nullity. We make ourselves nothing, a loser, in order to be seen as nothing - the ultimate protection against the necessity of existing and the obligation of being one's self.

It is from this that we get the simultaneous contradictory situation of not being seen and being perpetually visible. Everyone wants it both ways, and no legislation or ethics can get to the bottom of this dilemma - the unconditional right of being able to view and at the same time to not be viewed in return. Complete information access is part of human rights and with it we also find a forced visibility and over-exposure to the lighting of information.

Self-expression as the ultimate form of confession, as Foucault used to say. Keep no secrets. Speak, speak, and communicate endlessly. This is the type of violence aimed at the singular being and his secret. And at the same time, it is a form of violence against language as well, because from here on, it also loses its singularity, it is no longer anything but a medium, an operator of visibility, it completely loses its ironic and symbolic dimensions - precisely at the point where language becomes more important than what it says.

The worst part of this obscenity, this shameless visibility, is the forced participation, this automatic complicity of the spectator who has been blackmailed into participating. And it is this which is the clearest objective of the operation: the servitude of the victims, but a voluntary servitude, one in which the victims rejoice from the pain and shame which they are made to suffer. The complete participation of a society in its fundamental mechanism: interactive exclusion - it doesn't get better than that! Decided all together and consumed with enthusiasm.

If everything ends up being visible, (which is, like heat in the theory of energy, the most degraded form of existence) the crucial point nevertheless is to succeed in creating out of this extreme disenchantment of life, out of this loss of any symbolic space, an object of contemplation, of awe-struck observation and perverse desire. "Humanity which, beginning with Homer, once used to be the object of contemplation for the Gods, has now become the contemplation of itself. Its alienation from itself has reached such a point that humanity experiences its own destruction as an aesthetic sensation of the highest degree." (Walter Benjamin)

Everywhere, the experimental supersedes the real and the imaginary. Everywhere, it is the protocols of science and verification which have inoculated us, and we are in the middle, under the camera's scalpel, dissecting in vivisection the dimension of social relations, outside of any language or symbolic context. Catherine Millet as well is an example of the experimental - another kind of "vivisection": the entire sexual imaginary is swept away, all that remains is a perpetual protocol in the form of an unlimited verification of sexual functioning, a mechanism which in the end no longer has anything sexual about it.

There is a double misinterpretation:

- Making sexuality itself the ultimate reference. Repressed or expressed, sexuality is at best a hypothesis, and as such, it would be incorrect to make a reference or some sort of truth out of it. The sexual hypothesis is perhaps nothing more than a fantasy itself, and in any case, it is via repression that sexuality took on this authority and this aura of a strange attractor - and in its manifestation, it even loses this potential quality.

- From this we find the absurdity of acting out the systematic "liberation" of sex: one doesn't "liberate" a hypothesis. As for proving sex by sex, what a sad affair! As if everything was found within movement, derivation, transfer, and metaphor - It is not at all found within sex and desire, but within the filter of seduction, within the game where sex and desire are played with.

This is what renders the idea of showing "live sex" impossible. The same can be said for the viewing of "live" death or a "live" event on the news - all of these ideas are incredibly naturalistic. This is where we can see the pretension of bringing everything into the real world, of claiming that everything should be accelerated into an integral reality. And somewhere, we see, this is precisely the essence of power itself. "The corruption of power is to inscribe into the real everything which is found in dreams…."

The key to all of this is given to us by Jacques Henric in his conception of the image and photography: no use in covering one's face, our curiosity in regards to images has always been of a sexual order - all that we strive to locate within them, in the end, is sex, and more particularly feminine sex. And here not only do we find Courbet's

Origin of the World, but the origin of all images. So, let's go: let's photograph this one thing, let's give ourselves over to this singular scopic obsession! Such is the principle of a "real-erotik" of which the perpetual copulatory *acting-out* of Catherine Millet is the bodily equivalent: since in the end, what everyone dreams about is the unlimited sexual use of the body, let's go ahead and get right to the completion of this program!

No more seduction, no more desire, not even *jouissance* is spared. All that remains is the endless repetition, within an act of accumulation where quantity wins out over quality. A foreclosure of seduction. The lone question we have is the same one a man whispers into the ear of a woman during an orgy: *"what are you doing after the orgy?"* But this is also a useless question since for her there is no going beyond the orgy. She is

14

herself, in fact, beyond the end, where all processes take on an exponential allure and can only continue to indefinitely self-replicate. The same process is found in Alfred Jarry's *Supermale* (*Le Surmâle*), where, once the critical threshold has been reached, one can make love indefinitely. This is the automatic stage of the sexual machine. When sex has become nothing more than *sex processing,* it becomes transfinite and exponential. Nevertheless, it does not achieve its goal, which would be to exhaust sex itself, to go all the way to the end of the sexual exercise. This is obviously impossible. And this impossibility is all that remains of seduction and its revenge (and sexuality's revenge) against its unscrupulous operators - unscrupulous in regards to themselves and their own desire and pleasure.

"Think like a woman takes off her dress", says Bataille, but the naivety of all the

"Catherine Millets" of the world is thinking that taking off one's dress equates to being completely naked and that in doing so, one has access to the naked truth of sex and the world. If people take off their clothes, it is in order to be seen - not to be seen naked like truth (who still believes that truth remains truth once we have removed its veil?) but to be born into the realm of appearances, which is to say, the realm of seduction - and this is precisely the opposite of truth.

This modern disenchanted vision of the world, which considers the body as an object waiting to be undressed, and sex a desire merely waiting to be acted out and as pleasure to be fulfilled, is a complete misinterpretation. Whereas every culture based around masks, veils, and ornament says the exact opposite: they say the body is a metaphor. The real objects of desire and pleasure are the signs and marks

16

that pull the body away from its nudity, naturalness, its "truth", its integral reality of its physical being. Everywhere, it is seduction that tears things away from their truth, (including their sexual truth). And if thought takes off its dress, it is not in order to reveal itself in its nakedness, nor unveil the secret which up until that point would have been hidden. It would be in order to make this body appear as definitively enigmatic, secret, as a pure object whose mystery can never be revealed and which has no right being uncovered.

Under these conditions, the Afghan woman behind a Moucharaby lattice work, the woman covered in a sort of screen on the cover of *Elle* magazine, become striking alternative contrasts to the maddening virginal figure of Catherine Millet: The excess of the secret up against the excess of indecency. And yet, this indecency itself, this radical obscenity (like that found in *Loft Story*) is still a veil, the ultimate veil of veils - impossible to lift this final one, the one which imposes itself once we have thought we have lifted all the others. We would like to get a glimpse of the worst, the paroxysm of exhibition, achieve total nudity, absolute raw and violent reality - we never get there. And there is nothing to do about it - the wall of the obscene is impenetrable. Paradoxically, this lost quest allows all the better for the reemergence of the fundamental rule of the game: the rule of the sublime, the rule of the secret, seduction, including the rule which leads us to continually track without end those veils which have already been torn apart.

Why not propose a reverse hypothesis (to that of voyeurism and collective stupidity) that what people are searching for - every one of us - in colliding with the wall of obscenity, is to regain the feeling that there is nothing precisely to see, that we will never know the last word, and thus to verify *a contrario* the ultimate power of seduction? A desperate verification, but the experimental is always desperate. What *Loft Story* claims to verify is that the human being is a social being - which is not at all certain. What Catherine Millet claims to verify is that she is a sexed being - which is not certain either. What is verified in these experiments are the conditions themselves of experimentation, merely brought to their limit. The system decodes itself the best in its extravagances, but it is the same everywhere. Cruelty is the same everywhere. At the end of the day, to use a quote from Duchamp, it all amounts to "dust breeding".

TELEMORPHOSIS

The **problem with** *Loft Story* is three-fold: there is what happens in the Loft, which, in itself, is uninteresting, and, in contradiction with this insignificance, the immense fascination that it exerts. But this fascination is itself the object of fascination for the critical gaze. Where is the original event in all of this? There isn't one. All that remains is this mysterious contagion, this viral chain that functions from one end to the other, and to which we are all accomplices even in our analyses. It is useless to invoke all sorts of economic, political, and marketing data - the market is the market, and all commentaries themselves become part of the cultural and ideological market place. The mass effect is beyond manipulation, and incommensurate with the causes. This makes it exciting, like everything that resists intelligence.

The first hypothesis: if the audience is seen as such, it is not *in spite* of its stupidity, but thanks to this imbecility and the nullity of the spectacle. This seems to be quite certain. But this opens up two possibilities, which are perhaps not exclusive. Either the spectators immerse themselves within the void of the spectacle and get off from it like they do from their own image, everything merely provided with a face-lift for the circumstances, or they get off by feeling less idiotic than the spectacle - and thus never get tired of staring at it. This could perhaps be a media strategy to merely offer up spectacles that are more ridiculous than reality itself - hyperreal in their idiocy, and providing the spectators with a different possibility of satisfaction. A seductive hypothesis, but which pre-supposes a large imagination on the part of the creators of the shows. Thus, it's better to hold on to the presumption of nullity - in the same way one says the pre-sumption of innocence. And this, this is radical democracy. The democratic prin-ciple was of the order of merit, and equiv-alence (albeit relative) between merit and recognition. Here, in the Loft, there is no equivalence between merit and glory. It is everything in exchange for nothing. A complete principle of inequivalence. The democratic illusion is thus elevated to the highest degree: the maximal exaltation for a minimal qualification. And, while the traditional principle merely insured a partial recognition for merit, the operation of the Loft insures a virtual glory to everyone in terms of the absence of merit itself. On one hand, it is the end of democracy, by the extinction of any qualification of merit whatsoever, but on the other hand, it is the result of an even more radical democracy on the basis of the beatification of the man without qualities. It is a great step towards democratic nihilism.

In this disequilibrium between merit and public recognition, there is a kind of breakdown of the social contract which leads to another type of injustice and anomaly: while we could accuse traditional democracy of not rewarding their citizens with the merit they deserved, here one would be better off accusing it of indifferently overvaluing everyone on the basis of nothing. There is almost something funny and ferociously ironic about this strange glory devoted to anyone - because this form of radical democracy is a mockery of the entire establishment and its figures whether they are politicians, *intelligentsia,* or the *star system,* which make claim on some sort of glory based on their status or worth. At the least, this unfair competition of glory *start-ups* reveals both the latent imposture of all systems of distinction and the absurdity of a democracy embedded within a logic of the very worst. That being said, if these new exciting stars, emotionally intriguing thanks to their insignificance and transparency, if these usurpers produce an unbridled speculation against any egalitarian whole, if these *hit-parade* pirates do not deserve this glory excess, the society which permits itself to enjoy the enthusiastic spectacle of this masquerade deserves exactly what it gets. *Loft Story* is both the mirror and the disaster of an entire society caught up in the race towards meaninglessness and swooning in front of its own banality.

Here, television succeeded in completing a fantastic operation of directed consensus building, a real power grab, an OPA to the entire society, a kidnapping - an unheralded success story on the path towards an integral telemorphosis of society. Television created a global event (or better, a non-event), in which everyone became trapped. "A total social fact" as Marcel Mauss says - if in other societies this situation indicated the converging power of all the elements of the social, in our society it indicates the elevation of an entire society to the parody stage of an integral farce, of an image feedback relentless with its own reality. What the most radical critical critique, the most subversive delirious imagination, what no Situationist drift could have done... television has done.

Television has shown itself to be the strongest power within the science of imaginary solutions. But if television has achieved this, we are the ones who wanted it. There is no use in accusing the powers of media, or those of wealth, or even public stupidity in order to allow for some sort of hope of a rational alternative to this technical, experimental, and integral socialization in which we are all engaged, and which ends in the automatic coordination of individuals within irrevocable consensual processes. Let's call this the integral event of a society which, from then on, without a contract or rules, nor system of values other than a reflexive complicity, without any other rule or logic than that of immediate contagion of a promiscuity, blends us all together with an immense indivisible being. We've become individuated beings: non-divisible with others or ourselves. This individuation, which we are so proud of, has nothing to do with personal liberty; on the contrary, it is a general promiscuity. It is not necessarily a promiscuity of bodies in space - but of screens from one end of the world to the other. And it is probably screen promiscuity that is the real promiscuity: the indivisibility of every human particle at a distance tens of thousands of kilometers - like millions of twins who are incapable of separating from their double. Umbilicus limbo.

It can also be the promiscuity of a whole population with the extras from the Loft. Or even more, that of an "interactive" couple who continuously project the entirety of their relationship onto the Internet in real-time. Who watches them?

They watch themselves, but who else does, since everyone can get off, virtually speaking, from the same domestically integrated circuit? There will soon be nothing more than self-communicating zombies, whose lone umbilical relay will be their own feedback image - electronic avatars of dead shadows who, beyond death and the river Styx, will wander, perpetually passing their time retelling their own story. Just enough of something is still taking place in order to give the retrospective illusion, beyond the end, of reality - or, in the case of Catherine Millet, the illusion of sexuality - or the illusion of the social, but which is only evoked in a desperate interaction with oneself.

One of the signs of this promiscuity is the compulsion of confinement which we see flourishing everywhere - whether it is like the confinement seen in *Loft Story* or that of an island, a gated community, a luxury ghetto, or any space where people recreate in an experimental nest or privileged zone - some sort of equivalent space of initiation where the laws of open society are abolished. It is no longer about protecting a symbolic territory but of closing oneself off with one's own self-image, to live promiscuously with it as in a nest, in an incestuous complicity with it and with all the effects of transparency and feedback images which are those of a total screen, no longer having anything to do with others but via the relationship of image-to-image.

Moreover, the Loft could just as well have been fabricated with synthetic images - and in the future, it will be. But at the end of the day, they already are synthetic images. The gestures, the speeches, and actors already respond to the conditions of prefabrication, of programmed representation in the same way that in the future we will biologically clone human beings. But, in the end, they are already mentally and culturally profiles of clones.

This promiscuity made from mental involution and social implosion, but also from "on-line" interaction, this disavowal of any conflicting dimension whatsoever: is this an accidental consequence of the modern evolution of societies, or is it a natural condition of man, which will finally be able to put an end to the idea that man's social dimension of being is an artificial one? Is the human being a social being? It will be interesting to see if he continues as such in the future, as a being without a deep social structure, without a governed system of values and relations - within the pure contiguity and promiscuity of the networks, on automatic pilot, and in a kind of irreversible coma - and thus contrary to all presuppositions of anthropology. But, as Stanislaw

Lem tells us: do we not have too much of an anthropological conception of man?

In any case, seen by the success of *Loft Story* and the enthusiastic reception of this staging of experimental servitude, we can guess that the exercising of freedom is most certainly not a basic given in anthropology, and that man, if he ever did exercise freedom, never stops relinquishing it for the benefit of more animalistic techniques of collective automation. "If man does not do well with supporting the freedom of others, it is because it is not part of his nature. He does not even support this freedom for himself." (Dostoyevsky) But he adds something else to his servitude: the enjoyment of the spectacle of servitude.

Truth be told, the reality show itself quickly degenerated into a televisual soap opera that was not that different than old variety shows made for large audiences. And its audience was amplified at the usual rate of competing *media*, which leads to the self-propagation of the show via a prophetic method: *self-fulfilling prophecy*. In the end, the ratings for the show play part of the spiral and return cycle of the advertising flame. But all of this is of little interest. It is only the original idea which has any value: submitting a group to a sensory deprivation experiment[3], in order to record the behavior of human molecules within a vacuum - and no doubt with the design of watching them tear each other apart in the artificial promiscuity. We have not yet reached this point, but this existential micro-situation functions as a universal metaphor for the

---

3   Which in other times was a form of calculated torture. But are we not in the middle of exploring all the historical forms of torture, served in homeopathic doses, under the guise of mass culture or avant-garde art? This is precisely one of the principle themes of contemporary art.

modern being, holed up in his personal loft, which is no longer his physical or mental universe. It is his digital and tactile universe, of Turing's "spectral body", of the digital man, captured within the labyrinth of the networks, of man turned into his own (white) mouse.

The most remarkable thing about it all is providing this properly unbearable situation to the gaze of the crowds, getting them to relish the event as an orgy with no tomorrow. A beautiful exploit, but it won't end there. Soon, following the same logic, we will have *snuff films* and televised bodily torture. Death as well must logically enter onto the stage as an experimental event. Not at all in the form of a sacrifice - it is precisely at the same point in culture we are trying to technologically eliminate it, that it will make its return on the screens as an experience of the extreme (a foreseen revival by specific groups like those in trench warfare or the battles of the Pacific - still Disneyland but with a bit crueler infantilism). But at the same time, it returns as a pseudo-event, because - and this is the irony of all these experimental masquerades - parallel to the multiplication of these spectacles of violence grows the uncertainty in regards to the reality of what is being viewed. Did it or did it not take place? The more we advance into the orgy of the image and the gaze, the less we can believe it. "Real time" vision merely adds to the unreality of it. The two paroxysms: violence of the image and the discrediting of the image, cross paths according to the same exponential function. This leads us to constantly being doomed to deception (and more and more to the deception of synthetic images and CGI) but also revived by the deception itself. Because this profound uncertainty (strategically and politically determined - who else would profit from it?) is to a large degree part of the insatiable demand of this type of spectacle.

A dizzying curiosity mistaken for a voyeurism, but which in fact, in both the case of *Loft Story* and Catherine Millet, has nothing at all sexual about it. It is a curiosity of the visceral, organic and endoscopic order. This evokes the Japanese striptease where clients are invited to plunge their noses and gaze into the woman's vagina in order, apparently, to explore the secret of her entrails - something quite different in its fascination than sexual penetration. A speleological *jouissance* (not too different than the videoscopy of the internal body by micro-cameras), a gaping hole abyss of the entire body. This is not too different as well from the caliph who, after the dance of the stripper, cuts her open to find out just a bit more about what's underneath. Sex and sexual knowledge are superficial compared to this. The real bottomless curiosity is the one deep down. This compulsive involutive fetal gap that, to me appears to be in play in the so-called "sexual" activity of Catherine Millet and the fascination she exerts. Can one penetrate any further, even further than the sexual? Can one possess and be possessed completely?

It is, of course, an adventure without end. It can only come to an end via the countless repetitions of the sexual act, which nevertheless will never lead to absolute bodily knowledge nor the mortal pleasure of its exhaustion. In *Supermale* by Alfred Jarry, where Ellen and Marcueil flirt as well at the limits of sexual energy, Ellen dies (momentarily) at the achievement of this feat. There is nothing of the sort with Catherine Millet whose adventure is more of a kind of frustrated sexual anorexia. But, what is interesting, is that in pushing sex to an absurd position, to a seriality where it can no longer be defined as such except by its automatism (equal to Jarry's velocipedic cadavers who pedal their bicycles even better when they are dead), in ripping sex away from the pleasure principle itself, she also rips sex away from the reality principle and here as well forces the question to be posed: What happened to the sexual being? Would sexuality, contrary to all natural evidence, be merely a hypothesis? Verified here all the way until exhaustion, we have to wonder. Verified beyond its end, it simply no longer knows what it is…. Everything must be revised: with *Loft Story*, the evidence of the human being as a social being. With Catherine Millet, the evidence of the human being as a sexual being. With the abundance of transparency and information, the evidence of reality *tout court.*

Sexed (*sexués*), certainly we all are - and Catherine Millet as well, but sexual? This is the question.

Socialized, we are (and often by force) but social beings? That remains to be seen.

Realized, yes - but real? Nothing is less certain.

What Catherine Millet has in common with the people in the Loft is that she is subjected, by her own choice, via *serial fucking,* to the same sensory deprivation - giving way to the same radical, unique, minimal activity, which, by its repetition alone, becomes virtual. Not only does she get rid of any dual exchange or sexual participation, but also any obligation of orgasm or choice - and in the end she simply gets rid of her own body. We can see in this refusal of choice as with any sort of elective affinity, a type of asceticism, a flaying of free will (which we know, is merely a subjective illusion), which would make Catherine Millet, as some have said, a saint....

But what can we say about sexuality? It is surely a less illusory hypothesis than that of free will, but is it a good thing to put an end to it in verifying it with such ruthlessness? If doing away with desire and its concept can be characterized as a nihilism of will, then this reiterated proof of the existence of sex by sex can be considered as a sexual nihilism. Unless....

Unless the secret objective is to get rid of sex itself? To exhaust this mechanical function of bodies before getting around to the grand game.... Surely this is the underlying meaning of:

What are you doing after the orgy? Once the wager and performance have been made *(we did it!)* can we not get on to more serious things and really have some fun? Thus, according to Noëlle Châtelet, the true gastronome makes sure to eat before getting to the pleasure of sitting at the table, hunger should not burden her.

Ellen, after the sexual rally with Marcueil: "That was no fun at all", she says. Moreover, Marcueil compares the tetanic erection and the parallel state in women to a "sclerosis", or spasmodic contortion of tissues. Thus, in secret, Ellen invites him to begin again, but this time, "for pleasure's sake" (and without the expert eye of Bathybius, scientifically recording the feat).

If this reversal doesn't take place, what is there to do after the orgy? Nothing, unless, as in another of Jarry's texts, the hero from *Absolute Love,* Sengle, who right in the middle of an erotic act counts the number of times they have performed it and realizing he made a mistake exclaims, "Well, let's erase everything and start over!"

We find the same sensory deprivation in Catherine Millet as we do in *Loft Story,* the same attractive opening within the spectacle of the Loft as in the sexual offering of Catherine Millet. The same vaginal curiosity, more than vaginal, uterine even, for the hole in *Loft Story,* but in this instance opened up to another abyss: the void of insignificance. Always heading deeper towards this incontestable primitive scene of modernity. Where is the secret of banality, of this overexposed nullity, enlightened and informed from all sides, and which leaves nothing more to be seen except for transparency? The real mystery becomes what to make of this forced confession of life as such…. It is both the object of a veritable horror, and the dizzying temptation to plunge into this limbo - the limbo of an existence in a vacuum and stripped of all meaning: the spectacle itself that we offer up to the Loft and its actors.

The twentieth century has seen all sorts of crimes - Auschwitz, Hiroshima, geno-cides - but the lone true perfect crime, is, according to Heideggerian terms, "the second fall of man, the fall into banality".

There is a murderous violence of banal-ity that, precisely due to its indifference and its monotony, is the subtlest form of extermination. A veritable theatre of cruelty, of our cruelty to ourselves, completely played down and without a trace of blood. A perfect crime in that it abolishes all stakes and erases its own traces - but above all in so far as in this murder, we are both the murderers and the victims. As long as this distinction exists, the crime is not perfect. And yet in all historical crimes that we know of, the distinction is clear. It is only with suicide that the murderer and the victim become the same, and in this regard the immersion into banality is indeed the equivalent of the suicide of the species.

The other aspect of this murderous banality is that it erases the theatre of operations of the crime - it is from then on everywhere within life, on every screen, within the lack of distinction between life and the screen. Here as well, we find ourselves on both sides of the equation. And while the other violent crimes of history provided us with an image (*Shoah, Apocalypse Now*) which at least could be distinguished from the crime, with this other crime, this slow extermination offered up for our viewing pleasure via a spectacle like *Loft Story* and others, is one in which both *Loft Story* and ourselves all play a role.

We are dealing with a genuine Stockholm syndrome on a mass scale - when the hostage becomes the accomplice of the hostage taker - as well as a revolution of the concept of voluntary servitude and master-slave relations. When the entire society becomes an accomplice to those who took it hostage, but just as much when individuals split into, for themselves, hostage and hostage taker.

There is a long history of this growing promiscuity, from the glorification of daily life and its irruption within the historical dimension - up until the implacable immersion into the real all too real, into the human all too human, into the banal and residual. But the last decade saw an extraordinary acceleration of this banalization of the world, by the relay of information and universal communication - and above all by the fact that this banality has become experimental. The field of banality is no longer merely residual; it has become a theatre of operations. Brought to the screen, as is the case with *Loft Story,* it becomes an object of experimental leisure and desire. A verification of what Marshall McLuhan stated about television: that it is a perpetual test, and we are subjected to it like guinea pigs, in an automatic mental interaction.

But *Loft Story* is merely a detail. It is all of "reality" which has passed over to the other side like we see in the film *The Truman Show,* where not only is the hero telemorphosized, but everyone else involved as well - accomplices and prisoners caught in the spotlight of the same deception. There was a time - like in the film, *The Purple Rose of Cairo* - where the characters jumped off the screen and entered into real life in order to be embodied - a poetic situational reversal. Today, reality massively transfuses itself into the screen in order to become dis-embodied. Nothing any longer separates them. The osmosis, the telemorphosis, is total.

Pleasantville provided an opposite example of the heroic young couple of TV viewers who enter into the TV show and disrupt the direction of the show by reinjecting human passions into it (quite curiously, it is not sex which resuscitates life and brings back the color to an other-wise black and white world - the secret lies elsewhere). But all of this is just part of a running gag between the screen and reality which is over. Today, the screen is no longer the television screen;

it is the screen of reality itself - of what we can call integral reality. *Loft Story* is integral sociality. Catherine Millet is integral sexuality. The immanence of banality, the more real than real, is integral reality. By its absorption in information and the virtual, behind the murder underlying the pacification of life and the enthusiastic consumption of this hallucinogenic banality, reality is a process heading towards completion and it is lethal at every dimension. A return to limbo, to this crepuscular zone where, by its very realization, everything comes to an end.

Somewhere, we all mourn this stripped reality, this residual existence, this total disillusion. And there is, within this entire story of the Loft, a collective work of mourning. But a mourning which is part of the solidarity between the criminals themselves that we all are - the murderers of this crime perpetrated against real life, and the wallowing confession made to the screen, which in some ways becomes our literal confessional (the confessional is one of the key sites of *Loft Story*). Here we see our true mental corruption - in the consumption of this deception and mourning which becomes a contradictory source of pleasure. In any case, nevertheless, the disavowal of this experimental masquerade is reflected in the deadly boredom that emanates from it.

That being said, we cannot see why man would not claim his right to banality, insignificance, and nullity, and at the same time demand its opposite. After all, the right itself is part of the banalization of existence.

Integral sociality - integral sexuality - integral reality: this entire process would be catastrophic if there existed a truth of the social, a truth of the sexual, a truth of the real. Fortunately, they are merely hypotheses, and if today they take the form of a monstrous reality, they are nonetheless hypotheses. Forever unverifiable - the secret will never be uncovered. Truth, if it existed, would be that of sex. Sex would be the final word of this story…. But it isn't…. This is why sexuality will only ever be a hypothesis.

Meaning that the absolute of a systematic implementation of the social, a systematic implementation of the sexual, and a systematic operation of the real is itself, merely… virtual.

Hence the other question, taking the place as a final interrogation: WHO WAS LAUGHING IN THE LOFT? Within this material world without a trace of humor, what sort of monster could laugh back-stage? What sort of sarcastic divinity could laugh about all of it from his innermost depths? The human all too human must have turned over in his grave. But as we know very well, human convulsions are a distraction for the gods, who merely laugh at them.

Univocal Publishing
123 North 3rd Street, #202
Minneapolis, MN 55401
www.univocalpublishing.com

ISBN 9781937561000

Jason Wagner, Drew S. Burk
(Editors)

This work was composed in
Berkley and Block.

All materials were printed and bound
in September 2011 at Univocal's atelier
in Minneapolis, USA.

The paper is Mohawk Via Linen, Pure White.
The letterpress cover was printed
on Crane's Lettra Pearl.
Both are archival quality and acid-free.